M000281154

WEIMARANER:
THE WEIMARANER
BIBLE

Weimaraner Complete Guide

INCLUDES: WEIMARANER PUPPIES, WEIMARANER DOGS,
WEIMARANER RESCUE, BREEDERS,
WEIMARANER TEMPERAMENT, CARE, AND MORE!

By Susanne Saben

© DYM Worldwide Publishers

DYM Worldwide Publishers

ISBN: 978-1-911355-34-2

Internet. The accuracy and completeness of the information provided herein and opinions stated herein are not guaranteed or warranted to produce any particular results, and the advice or strategies, contained herein may not be suitable for every individual. The author, publisher, distributors, and/or affiliates shall not be liable for any loss incurred as a consequence of the use and application, directly or indirectly of any information presented in this work. This publication is designed to provide information in regards to the subject matter covered. The information included in this book has been compiled to give an overview of the topics covered. The information contained in this book has been compiled to provide an overview of the subject. It is not intended as medical advice and should not be construed as such. For a firm diagnosis of any medical conditions you should consult a doctor or veterinarian (as related to animal health). The writer, publisher, distributors, and/or affiliates of this work are not responsible for any damages or negative consequences following any of the treatments or methods highlighted in this book. Website links are for informational purposes only and should not be seen as a personal endorsement; the same applies to any products or services mentioned in this work. The reader should also be aware that although the web links included were correct at the time of writing they may become out of date in the future. Any pricing or currency exchange rate information was accurate at the time of writing but may become out of date in the future. The Author, Publisher, distributors, and/or affiliates assume no responsibility for pricing and currency exchange rates mentioned within this work.

Table of Contents

Resource List

This quality resource list will help you further maximize your experience with the Weimaraner breed. Enjoy!

Breeders USA (in alphabetical order):

- **Barrett Weimaraners**
  http://www.barrettweimaraners.com - USA Breeder, Based in Southern California

- **Blue Ridge Weimaraners**
  http://www.blueridgeweimaraners.com - USA Breeder, Based in Missouri, Family Business Great Story on Website.

- **BTW Kennels**
  http://www.btwkennels.com - USA Breeder, Based in Pennsylvania

- **Camelot Weimaraners**
  http://www.camelotweimaraner.com - USA Breeder, Based in Rhode Island, 30+ Years of Experience

- **Drehbar Weimaraners**
  http://www.drehbarweims.com - USA Breeder, Based in Michigan, AKC and UKC Registered.

- **Driftwood Weimaraners**
  http://driftwoodweimaraners.com USA Breeder, Based in North Carolina. Multiple Show Champions.

- **Foxfire Weimaraners**
  http://www.foxfireweims.com USA Breeder, Based in Colorado, Over 20 Years of Experience, AKC Breeder of Merit

- **HiBourne Weimaraners**

http://www.hibourne.com - USA Breeder, Based in New York, Champion Versatile Weimaraners Since 1984.

- **Indaba Weimaraners**
  http://www.indabaweimaraners.com - USA Breeder, Based in Maine, Family Business for Over 50 years.

- **Miller's Kennel**
  http://www.millerskennel.com - USA Breeder, Illinois Based Over 20 Years Experience with 2 Year Genetic Health Guarantee

- **Palm Coast Weimaraners**
  http://www.palmcoastweims.com - USA Breeder, Based in Florida

- **Regen Weimaraners**
  http://www.regen-weimaraners.com - USA Breeder, Based in Washington State, Multiple Top Champions in the Line.

- **Schwartz Family Weimaraners**
  http://schwartzfamilyweimaraners.com - USA Breeder, Based in Pennsylvania, Puppy and Stud Service, Many Details on Website.

- **Silverpoint Weimaraners**
  http://www.silverpointweimaraners.com - USA Breeder, Based in Kansas, Many Champions in the Line.

- **Silvershot Weimaraners**
  http://www.silvershotweimaraners.com - USA Breeder, Based in Michigan, Many Champions in the Line

- **Silversmith Farm**
  http://www.silversmithfarm.com - USA Breeder, Based in South Carolina, Many Champions in the Line.

- **Vega Weimaraners**
  http://www.vegaweim.com - USA Breeder, Based in Florida,

Member of ASPB.

- **Willow Ridge Weimaraners**
  http://www.willowridgeweimaraners.com - USA Breeder,
  Based in Kentucky, Many Positive Testimonials on Site.

- **Wire Grass Weimaraners**
  http://www.wiregrassweimaranerstoo.com - USA Breeder,
  Florida Based.

- **Wyheestar Weimaraners**
  http://www.owyheestar.com - USA Breeder, Oregon based,
  Family Based Business

BREEDERS CANADA:

- **Bartland Weimaraners**
  http://www.bartlandweimaraners.com - Canada Breeder,
  based in British Columbia, Over 20 Years Experience,
  Multiple Champions in Line.

- **Prairie Shadow Weimaraners**
  http://www.prairieshadowdogs.com - Canada Breeder, Based
  in Alberta, Many Details on Website

BREEDERS UK:

- **Minstergate Weimaraners**
  http://www.minstergate-weimaraners.org.uk - UK Breeders,
  Based in York, Over 25 Years of Experience.

- **Kalimor Weimaraners**
  http://kalimorweimaraners.co.uk - UK Breeders,
  Hertfordshire, Kennel Club Assured Breeder.

BREED SPECIFIC FURTHER RESOURCES:

"Breed Standard." - The Kennel Club. http://www.thekennelclub.org.uk/services/public/breed/standard.aspx?id=2058

"Brief History of the Weimaraner Breed." - Weimaraner Club of America. http://weimaranerclubofamerica.org

"Chewy.com" – http://www.chewy.com USA Site, Great selection of extremely tough chew toys, search "Kong" brand for your Weimaraner on the site.

"JeffersPet.com" – http://www.jefferspet.com Extensive Tough Toys and other Supplies, look for Kong brand.

"Most Popular Dog Breeds in America & Weimaraner Breed Standards" - http://www.akc.org/ American Kennel Club.

"Weimaraner Breed Standard." - Weimaraner Club of America. http://weimaranerclubofamerica.org

"The Weimaraner Breed. - Weimaraner Club of Great Britain." http://www.weimaraner.me.uk/index.php/the-breed

"Westpawdesign.com" – http://www.westpaw.com - Check out the extremely tough "Tux" toys for your Weimaraner.

CHAPTER 1

Introducing The Weimaraner

When you see a Weimaraner dog there is no way to confuse it for another breed. Sometimes nicknamed "the Gray Ghost," these dogs have an unmistakable silver-gray coat that sometimes exhibits a bluish sheen. In addition to their coat color, Weimaraners are also easy to identify by their long legs, lithe bodies, and large floppy ears. From the very first time you see a Weimaraner, this is not a breed you will soon forget!

I distinctly remember the first time I saw a Weimaraner. I was hiking through the woods at a park near my house, enjoying the cool weather as summer transitioned into fall. I was coming around a bend in the trail when I saw a mystical grey creature come bursting through the brush, running right toward me. I stopped in my tracks, mesmerized by the beauty of the thing and was still in a bit of shock when the creature came right up to me and I realized that I was being greeted by one of the most beautiful dogs I had ever seen.

As the dog nuzzled my hands and sniffed me over, his owner came around the bend, apologizing for his dog being so forward. I dismissed the apology and immediately began peppering him with questions about his beautiful dog. What breed was he? Where did he come from? How could I find one for myself!

The Weimaraner is a skilled hunting dog with versatile applications for pointing, tracking, and more.

It may sound crazy to you, but as soon as that dog shoved his wet nose into my outstretched hand, I knew I had to have one. After the dog's owner answered all of my questions I let him go and I finished my hike, all the while thinking about what I was going to name my Weimaraner when I got one. Following that encounter, it was only a matter of a few weeks before I had sought out a local Weimaraner breeder and put a deposit down on a puppy of my own. And that's how I came to be the proud owner of a gorgeous female Weimaraner named Misty.

The Weimaraner is a medium to large-breed dog that weighs up to 90 pounds but they are still very lean and muscular. These dogs are skilled at hunting a variety of prey animals but they can also make good family pets. Weimaraners are absolutely gorgeous with their silver-gray coats and their intelligence means that each and every day you share with your dog will bring something new. These dogs love to work and play, so be prepared to be an active dog owner and make sure your Weimaraner gets the training and socialization he needs from a young age!

The Weimaraner is easy to identify with his silver-gray coat, lean build, and large floppy ears.

If you are reading this book, then I think it is safe to say that you have your own curiosity about the Weimaraner breed much like I did. Some of you may already be familiar with the Weimaraner breed while others are just meeting the breed for the first time. No matter where you fall on the spectrum you have come to the right place for Weimaraner information! Though I have only had my Misty for three years now, I have learned a lot about the breed and I am anxious to share my knowledge and experience with you!

If you work to maintain a healthy relationship with your Weimaraner, he will become your lifelong friend and companion.

Before you can decide if the Weimaraner is the right breed for you, I want you to take the time to learn as much as you can about Weimaraner dogs. As beautiful as these dogs are, they aren't the right pet for everyone – they are very active and they require a great deal of mental and physical stimulation daily. These dogs are highly intelligent and they do not do well when left alone for long periods of time – they are not a low-maintenance breed.

Although raising and caring for a Weimaraner is hard work, I believe that it is well worth the effort. Weimaraners are beautiful, loving dogs that have the capacity to bond closely with family if you have the time to devote to their care. You should also be warned that these dogs tend to be a bit mischievous and they are talented escape artists! They also do not do well in apartments or condos because they need outdoor space to stretch their legs. If you have a decent-sized house and a fenced yard, you are golden!

Weimaraner puppies are full of energy and the love to play!

There is a great deal more that you need to learn about the Weimaraner dog before you think about looking for Weimaraner puppies. In this book, I will cover all the most important information about Weimaraners that you need to know. I'll give you a brief history of the dog breed Weimaraner as well as some general information about Weimaraner puppies and Weimaraner mix breeds. I'll also go into detail about feeding, grooming, and training.

Weimaraners are gorgeous and intelligent dogs – there is no denying that. But some of the traits that make them so unique also make them a challenge to keep. You will find may Weimaraner books out there, but this one is designed to be as detailed and as comprehensive as possible to ensure that you become the best Weimaraner owner you can be. By the time you finish reading this book, you will know whether the Weimaraner breed is right for you and, if it is, you will have the information you need to find Weimaraner puppies!

So, with all of that in mind, I want to thank you for buying this book! It was my goal to create the complete Weimaraner guide book for prospective dog owners like you. If you are ready to learn more about the gorgeous Weimaraner breed, just turn the page and keep reading!

CHAPTER 2

Weimaraner Dogs: The History of the Breed

H ave you ever taken a good hard look at a Weimaraner dog and wondered where it came from? Although the Weimaraner is similar in body structure to other pointing breeds, its blue-grey coat sets it apart from all the rest. I like to think that this breed has a touch of angelic beauty but I may be biased because my own Weimaraner is a perfect little angel. Each Weimaraner is unique, however, so to get a better understanding of the breed as a whole you need to learn about the breed's history.

The Development of the Dog Breed Weimaraner

According to the Weimaraner Club of America, the first specimens of the Weimaraner breed appeared during the 19th century at the Weimar court in Germany. These dogs were developed as versatile hunting dogs, skilled in tracking and known for their speed, agility, courage, and dependability. Early Weimaraner breeding programs were focused on developing these traits, not paying any particular attention to physical traits. Many researchers believe that the now iconic blue-gray coat that most

Weimaraners exhibit came about by accident.

Some researchers believe that the Weimaraner's iconic blue-gray coat came about by accident while the breed was in development.

It remains unclear exactly how the Weimaraner breed came about, though it is commonly believed that certain breeds played a role in the breed's development. Some of these breeds include the English Pointer, the Bloodhound, the German Shorthaired Pointer, and the blue Great Dane. As decades came and went, the forests in Germany shrank and large game became scarce. In order to preserve the Weimaraner breed, handlers began to develop the breed's hunting talents for smaller game such as rabbits, birds, and foxes. This may account for the versatility for which the Weimaraner breed is still known today.

In the year 1897, an exclusive breed club was formed in Germany with the goal of maintaining and developing the breed according to specific standards. Ownership of Weimaraner dogs was restricted to members of the club and strict guidelines were imposed on those who wanted to breed Weimaraners. This practice continued until in 1929, an American sportsman named Howard Knight, applied for membership to the German breed club and was granted admission – he was also given permission to bring two Weimaraners to the United States. However, because the club was overprotective of the breed, they gave him two de-sexed dogs that could not breed.

Despite this setback, Knight was not deterred – he kept working and eventually achieved his goal in 1938 when he acquired three female Weimaraner puppies and one male puppy. As Knight's success became known, other American breeders joined him and the Weimaraner Club of America was formed in 1942. The American Kennel Club (AKC) recognized the breed at the end of that year and the breed made its formal debut at the Westminster Kennel Club show the following year, in 1943.

Over the next few years as World War II raged oversees, it became difficult for German breeders to keep their dogs. Thus, many quality specimens of the Weimaraner breed were sent to the U.S. When the war ended, many American servicemen brought Weimaraners home with them which further contributed to the breed's growth in popularity. In fact, President Dwight D. Eisenhower even brought a Weimaraner into the White House – her name was Heidi.

By the mid-1950s, the dog Weimaraner had become the 12th most popular breed in the U.S. Unfortunately, the sudden increase in popularity led to some irresponsible breeding which reduced the quality of the breed and introduced some temperament problems. By the 1960s, the Weimaraner breed had declined such that registrations were cut in half and they kept decreasing through to the 1980s. Dedicated Weimaraner breeders continued working to improve the breed; and once again, registrations increased in the 1990s. Today, the Weimaraner is ranked among the top 30 breeds according to AKC registration statistics.

Weimaraners were originally developed for hunting large game but they are now a versatile gun dog and skilled hunter.

CHAPTER 3

Weimaraner Dog Types and Weimaraner Mix Dogs – The Long Haired Weimaraner and More!

While the Weimaraner is one of the most recognizable dog breeds out there with its silver-gray coat, there are some variations on the Weimaraner breed that you should be aware of. For example, some Weimaraners have a distinctly blue or brown coat rather than the typical silver-gray color. You may also come across Weimaraner mix breeds or even something called a Toy Weimaraner. In this chapter, I'll provide you with all of the information you need to know about Weimaraner dog types.

Variations on the Weimaraner – Blue Weimaraner, Long Haired Weimaraner and Weimaraner Brown Dogs

The Weimaraner's coat is short and sleek with a smooth texture – it also comes in a solid color, though it may fade to lighter shades on the ears and head. Most Weimaraners are solid gray in color with a dark gray nose, pink lips, and medium-sized round eyes in shades of amber, gray or blue-gray. It is possible for a Weimaraner to be born with a blue coat rather than a gray one. Blue Weimaraner puppies have a charcoal-gray colored coat which may vary in tone. In terms of genetics, a blue Weimaraner is a dilute black, and one parent must be a blue Weimaraner.

You may also be interested to know the truth about Weimaraner brown coloration. The traditional gray color for which the Weimaraner is known is actually a dilute brown. The shade varies from one dog to another depending on its breeding, and some dogs have a silvery sheen to their coat.

A long haired Weimaraner has silky smooth hair with feathering on the tail and legs.

There is some debate on the matter, but many historians believe that the shorthair Weimaraner and the long haired Weimaraner have been part of the breed's genetics since its initial development. A longhaired Weimaraner is the product of a recessive gene – this means that two shorthair parents can bear longhaired puppies. If a long haired Weimaraner is bred to a shorthair Weimaraner, however, all the puppies will have short hair but they will all carry the recessive longhair gene. Long haired Weimaraners have smooth, silky coats with feathering on the legs and tail.

Although blue Weimaraner dogs and long haired Weimaraner dogs exist, they are not accepted for registration or show with the American Kennel Club (AKC). The Weimaraner Club of America follows the same standard which excludes all colors except for solid gray in shades from mouse-gray to silver-gray. The same is true for the Kennel Club in the U.K. When it comes to the long haired Weimaraner, however, this variety IS recognized in the U.K., though it is rare.

The blue Weimaraner is a beautiful dog, even if its color is not accepted by the American Kennel Club for show.

If you are interested in learning more about the blue Weimaraner, you can find plenty of helpful information from the Blue Weimaraner Club of America.

Does the Toy Weimaraner Exist?

Many people love the Weimaraner breed but they simply don't have the space to dedicate to such a large dog. For this reason, there is some demand out there for a toy Weimaraner or a smaller version of the breed. What you need to realize, however, is that the Weimaraner is a medium- to large-breed dog that weighs anywhere from 55 to 90 pounds at maturity. Even if you were to breed Weimaraners down in size, they would still be a medium- to large-sized breed.

If you come across a toy Weimaraner when looking for Weimaraner puppies for sale, you need to be very careful – because there is no actual breed called the toy Weimaraner. What you are seeing is probably just a Weimaraner puppy or a Weimaraner mix. There is nothing wrong with Weimaraner mix breeds, but you should be aware of the differences between a purebred Weimaraner and a Weimaraner mix.

Weimaraner Lab Mix and Other Weimaraner Mix Breeds

A Weimaraner mix is simply a Weimaraner dog crossed with another dog breed. When this kind of crossing is done intentionally, the resulting breed is often called a "designer dog". This is the trendy term but, in reality, these dogs are nothing more than mixed breeds. This isn't necessarily a bad thing, however – sometimes you can customize a dog to your individual preferences through careful crossbreeding. You must remember, however, that it is impossible to predict which traits the puppies will receive from either parent; you cannot completely control the outcome with Weimaraner mix breeds.

*The Weimaraner Lab mix is simply a crossing of the
Weimaraner breed and the Labrador Retriever.*

Theoretically, the Weimaraner can be bred with any other dog to create a Weimaraner mix. One of the most popular crossings, however, is the Weimaraner Lab mix. This is the result of crossing a purebred Weimaraner with a purebred Labrador Retriever. Both breeds are skilled hunters, so the resulting Weimaraner Lab mix will likely be talented in that area as well. You should be mindful, however, of the fact that both breeds are also very active, intelligent, and mischievous – crossing the two could cause these traits to become even more fully developed.

CHAPTER 4

Is The Weimaraner
the Right Dog For Me?

An Overview of Weimaraner Temperament, Weimaraner Training, and More

I love my Misty with all of my heart, but being a dog owner – particularly a Weimaraner owner – does have its challenges. Before you truly decide whether this is the breed for you, take the time to learn some of the practical aspects of being a Weimaraner owner. This includes learning about the breed's needs for exercise and space as well as learning the basics about the Weimaraner temperament. You should also brush up on dog training tips and puppy training tips because, in addition to being your Weimaraner's owner, you will also be his dog trainer. You will learn about these things and more in this chapter!

Weimaraner Space and Exercise Needs – Are They Easy to Keep?

The Weimaraner is generally considered a medium – to large-breed dog that weighs 55 to 90 pounds (25 to 41 kg) at maturity. This being the case, Weimaraner dogs generally do not do well in apartment or condo settings – they need a lot of space. Not only do these dogs need plenty of indoor space to play, they also require frequent access to the outdoors where they can run and work off some of their energy. Believe me, Weimaraners have an endless supply of energy!

In addition to being a medium to large-sized breed, the Weimaraner is also a hunting breed. Weimaraners have a strong desire to work so, even if you don't train your dog for hunting, I strongly recommend that you consider dog sports to teach your dog some discipline and to make sure that he gets the exercise he needs. Just be sure to supervise him any time he is outside because Weimaraners are talented escape artists – they are too clever for their own good!

Weimaraners are very active dogs that require a good deal of daily attention and exercise as well as outdoor space to play.

What some Weimaraner books fail to make clear is that not only does the Weimaraner breed need plenty of space and exercise – they also need a lot of attention. Weimaraners are a very social and people-oriented breed, so you should not be surprised if your dog follows you around the house. These dogs are highly prone to separation anxiety as well, so they don't do well when left alone for long periods of time. To help reduce the risk for separation anxiety and to keep your dog's energy under control, you should spend as much time as you can playing with your dog and cultivating a strong bond.

Weimaraner Temperament – Are They Family Dogs?

What many people remember most about the Weimaraner dog breed is their beautiful silver-blue coats. While the Weimaraner certainly is an attractive dog breed, there are so many more lovable qualities worth mentioning! For example, Weimaraner dogs are loving, affectionate, and loyal to a fault. They love to be around people (especially their owners) and they are highly social dogs. This breed needs a lot of daily attention in addition to exercise to maintain his physical and mental health.

Weimaraners are some of the most people-oriented dogs you will ever encounter. Sometimes I call my Misty "my little shadow" because she is always behind me, no matter where I go. The Weimaraner breed are extremely devoted to their families which can be unnerving for some people, but it is great if you want a dog who will never leave your side. These dogs are very friendly and quick to make friends as well.

In addition to being very friendly and people-oriented, the

Weimaraner dog breed is also very intelligent. These dogs are very smart which is good news when it comes time for training a Weimaraner – they learn quickly and are eager to please. Some Weimaraners, however, develop an independent streak which can make dog training a challenge. As long as you are firm and consistent with your dog however, you should be fine as a dog trainer. You will receive more information about how to train a dog later in this chapter and later in this book.

Another important aspect of the Weimaraner's temperament is their love for children. These dogs would never do anything to hurt anyone – child or animal – but they can be a little rambunctious at times, so supervise any interactions between your dog and your kids. If you want a dog that will love your kids and enjoy playing with them, however, the Weimaraner is a great choice.

Weimaraner dogs are some of the friendliest, most people-oriented dogs you will ever meet. They are smart too!

Weimaraner Dogs and Other Pets –
Do They Get Along?

Weimaraner training books are a great place to learn about
the personality and temperament of the Weimaraner breed.
The more you learn about the breed's temperament, the
better you will be able to understand what it is like to own a
Weimaraner. One thing many pet parents are concerned about
is whether Weimaraners get along with other dogs and pets. The
Weimaraner is a hunting breed, but they are surprisingly good
with other pets.

Although the Weimaraner was developed for hunting, these
dogs have a gentle and friendly temperament that makes for
an excellent family pet. Weimaraners are eager to make new
friends – animal or human – and you can always count on them
to be sociable. Weimaraners get along very well with other
dogs, though they sometimes display dominant or independent
tendencies. They can also get along with cats and other small
pets, especially when raised with them from a young age. Again,
however, you should supervise interactions just to be safe.

What Should You Know About Training
a Weimaraner?

For the most part, Weimaraner training books agree that
this breed is very smart and highly trainable. The smarter a
dog is, the easier he is to train. Do you want to know why?
At its most basic level, dog training is two-fold. For one
thing, it is about teaching your dog to correlate a specific
command with a specific behavior. Second, it is about

teaching your dog to exhibit the desired behavior on command. It is as simple as that!

Training a Weimaraner is generally fairly easy because the breed's intelligence means that they are quick to make that connection between the command and the desired behavior. If you praise and reward your dog for responding to the command appropriately, you will reinforce that response and your dog will be more likely to respond correctly in the future. The key to training a Weimaraner is to keep your training sessions short and sweet and to maintain a firm and consistent hand in leadership.

Owning a Weimaraner is a wonderful thing, but it can also be a challenge – make sure you are up to the task before you buy a Weimaraner puppy or adopt a Weimaraner dog!

Can You Handle a Weimaraner Dog?

Now that you know a little more about the Weimaraner breed you should have a pretty good idea whether or not this is the right breed for you. If you think that it is, congratulations! I am so excited for you! My life changed the day I brought my Misty home and I have never regretted having her by my side.

As wonderful as my Misty is, and as much as I enjoy being a dog owner, I must recognize that there are some challenges involved. Being a dog owner is time-consuming and expensive – it is not something you enter into lightly! Before you commit to a Weimaraner puppy, consult the following checklist to make sure that you have what it takes to be a Weimaraner owner:

Weimaraner Owner Checklist		
Do I have a large enough home to house a Weimaraner?	Yes	No
Do I have a fenced backyard or other safe outdoor space for my Weimaraner to play?	Yes	No

Do I have the time to devote to my Weimaraner every day?	Yes	No
Am I willing and able to train my Weimaraner from a young age?	Yes	No
Will I be patient with my Weimaraner as he learns?	Yes	No
Can I commit to feeding my Weimaraner a high-quality dog food?	Yes	No
Can I afford to take my dog to the vet twice a year for check-ups and vaccines?	Yes	No
Can I commit to keeping my Weimaraner for his whole life?	Yes	No

CHAPTER 5

Weimaraner Puppies For Sale—

Should You Buy a Weimaraner Puppy or Adopt from a Weimaraner Rescue?

B efore you get caught up in the excitement of finding your Weimaraner you need to think carefully about your options. Buying a Weimaraner for sale might be as easy as paying a visit to your local pet store, but that is probably not the best option. In this chapter, you will learn the basics about finding Weimaraner puppies for sale and receive some tips if you are considering adoption.

Weimaraner Puppies for Sale – Puppy or Adult Dog?

The first thing you need to ask yourself is whether you want an adult Weimaraner dog or a Weimaraner puppy. There are pros and cons for both of these options and you should think carefully before you decide.

When it comes to Weimaraner puppies, there are many benefits it comes but also some serious challenges. For one thing, Weimaraner puppies are just about the cutest things in the world – they are small and wriggly with giant floppy ears and big, sad eyes. Not only are puppies cute, but if you buy a Weimaraner puppy you have the opportunity to raise it and train it in whatever way you see fit. Starting with a puppy is also a great idea if you have other household pets that you want to get along with your dog.

Weimaraner puppies grow up into beautiful, athletic dogs with floppy ears, big hearts, and endless energy.

As for the downsides associated with Weimaraner puppies, they can be a lot of work but that is true of all puppies. It takes several weeks to housetrain a puppy and you may also have to deal with destructive behavior while your puppy learns the house rules. Training and socializing your puppy can be time-consuming and it may be more expensive to buy a puppy and to pay for all the puppy costs (like puppy shots and spay/neuter surgery) than to adopt an adult dog. You also have to gamble a little bit with a Weimaraner puppy in terms of temperament because a puppy's personality can change as he grows.

When it comes to adult Weimaraner dogs, there are some great benefits to consider. For example, adult dogs are fully developed in terms of their personality so, for the most part, what you see is what you get. If you get an adult dog, there is also a good chance that he will already be housetrained and may have some obedience training under his belt as well. You are also probably going to pay less in adoption fees for an adult dog than you would to buy a puppy and the dog may already be spayed or neutered if you get him from a shelter.

Though there are many benefits to getting an adult dog versus a puppy, there are some things that you will miss out on. For example, you won't get to experience the goofiness of a Weimaraner puppy as he experiences the world for the first time. You may not be able to influence his temperament or personality as much either, depending how old the adult dog is when you get him. Some adult dogs (especially shelter dog) also come from bad living situations which could mean behavioral problems.

To review the pros and cons for adult Weimaraner dogs versus Weimaraner puppies, consult the chart below:

Weimaraner Puppy	
Pros	Cons
Cute and cuddly	Can be destructive

You can influence his personality/temperament	Personality may change as he grows/develops
You get to train him in whatever way you want	Training and socialization takes time and patience
May form a stronger bond	More expensive to buy a puppy and pay for vaccines and spay/neuter surgery

Adult Weimaraner Dog	
Pros	**Cons**
Personality is largely set, won't change much	May come from a bad living situation – could mean behavioral issues
Less worry about destructive "puppy" behavior	May have some bad habits that need to be addressed
Already housetrained and may have some obedience training as well	You may not be able to influence his personality or temperament
May be spayed/neutered and caught up on vaccines	You miss out on cute puppy behavior
Less expensive than buying from a breeder	

Should You Buy a Puppy Weimaraner for Sale or Adopt from a Weimaraner Rescue?

Now that you've decided whether you want a Weimaraner puppy or a Weimaraner adult, your next step is to decide whether you want to go through a breeder or a Weimaraner rescue. If you are looking for Weimaraner puppies for sale, your best bet is to probably go with an independent breeder. Local dog rescue operations cannot guarantee that they will have any Weimaraner dogs for adoption at all, let alone puppies. It is also important to note that when it comes to the dog pound or dog rescue, puppies for adoption tend to go very quickly.

If you buy a Weimaraner puppy from a breeder you can influence his personality to some degree based on how you raise your puppy – training and socialization is important as well.

If you decide to adopt a dog from an animal rescue or Weimaraner rescue, you should be prepared to jump through a few hoops. You'll need to fill out an application with your contact information, proof of residency, proof that you are allowed to have pets at your residence and, in some cases, proof of income. There is also no guarantee that your application will be approved or that it will be chosen for the dog you are trying to adopt. On the flip side, adopting a Weimaraner is probably going to be much less costly than Weimaraner puppies for sale from a breeder.

The main benefit of going through a breeder when it comes to Weimaraner puppies is that you get to pick the exact puppy you want. It is important to note that puppies will change a little bit in terms of their temperament and personality as they grow and develop but, as the dog owner, you can influence that a little bit with the way you train and socialize your Weimaraner. Weimaraner puppies are absolutely adorable and they are smart so they generally learn pretty quickly.

If you want to support a local animal rescue shelter by adopting a Weimaraner, take the time to do your research. Find out how many dog shelters are in your area and find out if there are any local or regional rescue operations that specialize in Weimaraners. When looking for shelter dogs you may want to consider adopting from a high-kill shelter because the dogs there are at risk for being euthanized if they aren't adopted within a certain time frame. By adopting from one of these shelters, you will literally be saving a life.

Buying Blue Weimaraner Puppies?

When you are shopping for Weimaraner puppies for sale, you may come across blue Weimaraner puppies. But what is the difference between a blue Weimaraner and a gray Weimaraner? It is all about the coat and the tone of its color. When it comes to genetics, blue Weimaraner puppies are dilute blacks while gray Weimaraner puppies are dilute browns. The gene for blue color is dominant, so in order to have blue Weimaraner puppies you need only one blue Weimaraner parent.

Blue Weimaraner puppies has a distinctly beautiful charcoal-gray coat that almost has a bluish sheen to it.

If you are concerned about the color of your Weimaraner's coat, you need to be careful about where you get your puppy. Any responsible Weimaraner breeder will be able to tell you whether their puppies are blue or gray and you should be able to confirm those claims by looking at the parents. If a breeder has blue Weimaraner puppies for sale, at least one of the parents has to be a blue Weimaraner – you should receive visual confirmation by seeing the parent dogs and you should ask for the dog's pedigree as well.

CHAPTER 6

How to Avoid Buying Weimaraner Puppies Bred in Puppy Mills

A ccording to recent statistics, there are as many as 10,000 (or more) puppy mills in the United States alone. In the U.K., it is estimated that one out of three dogs sold comes from a puppy mill. But what exactly is a puppy mill, and why are they bad? Keep reading to learn more about puppy mills and why you should avoid them.

Picture this:

A young student responds to an online ad calling for a driver to transport puppies from a breeding facility to a local pet store. The student arrives at the location to make the pick-up – the time is 5 AM and it is a cold January morning. As soon as he steps out of the car, he notices a horrible smell emanating from the building. The student pauses for a moment then enters the building.

The building is large and metal – like an airplane hangar but instead of housing airplanes, it is filled with rows upon rows of wire kennels. Not only are the kennels taking up every inch of available floor space, but they are stacked on top of each other, six or seven high. Into each kennel three or four puppies are crammed – puppies of all different breeds and all very young, less than 8 weeks old.

The student pushes down his disgust and helps to load the puppies into the back of the van. In the van, the puppies are crammed into kennels that are too small and the puppies themselves are also small and very young – young enough that the student questions whether they are really ready to be separated from their mother. But he doesn't ask any questions. He gets into the driver's seat and starts to drive. Hours later, he arrives at the pet store to make his delivery.

Every year, thousands of puppies are born into squalid conditions to dogs that have never breathed fresh air.

This story is based on an account told by Josiah Hesse, a

writer for VICE online and it clearly depicts the horror of puppy mills. A puppy mill is a type of dog breeding facility where profit is king. Dogs are kept in squalid conditions with no room to move or exercise. They spend the majority of their lives in cramped kennels, suffering from malnutrition, disease, and exhaustion due to repetitive forced breeding. When a dog is no longer capable of breeding, she is put down and replaced by another dog.

If you are learning about puppy mills for the first time, you may find yourself thinking "That would never happen where I live," but you might be surprised. According to the American Kennel Club, 1.8 million puppies are sold each year in the U.S. that come from puppy mills. There are roughly 10,000 puppy mills in the United States and the number doesn't seem to be decreasing. For every puppy mill that is raided and shut down, another one rises to take its place.

What can you do to help rid the world of puppy mills? For one thing, you can refuse to support local pet stores that get their pets from puppy mills. Some pet stores get their puppies from local shelters and rescue organizations but many do not. If the pet store cannot tell you which breeder or organization the puppies came from, it is highly likely that they are the product of puppy mill breeding. Something else you can do to help is to contact your local legislators about your concerns.

CHAPTER 7

Weimaraner Breeders –

How Do You Find a Responsible Breeder With a Healthy Weimaraner for Sale?

If you have decided that you want a Weimaraner puppy, congratulations! You are going to fall in love with your new Weimaraner puppy immediately – I sure did with mine! But before you get caught up in the excitement about your new Weimaraner puppy, you need to think carefully about which breeder you are going to buy from. There are Weimaraner breeders all over the world but not all of them are responsible. In this chapter, you will learn how to find a responsible breeder and how to pick out a healthy Weimaraner puppy from a litter.

Finding a Responsible Weimaraner Breeder

When you are ready to start looking for Weimaraner puppies for sale, you should start by finding a list of breeders from your local, regional, or national Weimaraner breed club. In the United States, try the Weimaraner Club of America (WCA). For U.K. residents, try the Weimaraner Club of Great Britain. If none of these options presents a list of breeders that are close enough for you to consider, try doing an online search for Weimaraner breeders or

Weimaraner rescue operations. Whatever you do, don't buy Weimaraner puppies from a website that sells puppies online and ships them to you – these websites usually get their puppies from puppy mills.

If you have your heart set on a Weimaraner puppy, take the time to research responsible breeders in your area to make sure that the puppy you bring home is well-bred and in top condition.

Once you have collected a list of viable Weimaraner breeders, you need to go down the list and qualify each breeder to see if it is really a good option to consider. Start by checking the website for each breeder to get a feel for them – where are they located? How long have they been breeding dogs? Do they hold any certifications or licenses? Don't forget to look for reviews and recommendations of the breeders on your list.

After you've gotten a first impression of the breeders on

your list you can remove any that don't sound like good options. With your shortened list, you can take your investigation a little bit deeper. Come up with a list of questions and then contact each breeder by phone to ask those questions – their answers will help you to decide if they should stay on your list or be removed. Here are some sample questions you might ask:

- How long have you been breeding dogs? What about Weimaraners in particular?

- What do you love the most about the Weimaraner dog breed?

- What made you decide to start breeding Weimaraner dogs?

- How do you choose your breeding stock? What kind of genetic testing do you do?

- Do your Weimaraner puppies for sale come with any kind of health guarantee?

- Do you sell blue Weimaraner puppies, gray Weimaraner puppies, or both?

- How much do you charge for your puppies and how much of a deposit do you require?

As you talk to each breeder and get the answers to these questions, remove any breeder from your list that doesn't seem to be highly experienced and qualified. You should also pay attention to whether the breeder asks you any questions about yourself – a responsible breeder will take the time to get to know potential buyers because they want to make sure that their puppies go to good homes. After talking to each breeder, narrow down your list.

With the final two or three breeders on your list, you should seriously consider paying a visit to the breeding facilities before making your final decision. If you do, ask for a tour of the facilities and ask to see the parent dogs as well as the Weimaraner puppies for sale. If the facilities are not kept clean or the breeding stock isn't in prime condition, you probably shouldn't purchase a puppy from that breeder. If you are happy with what you see, however, you can move on to talks about how to reserve a puppy.

To help you narrow down your list of options for Weimaraner breeders, use this breeder report card to record the results of your investigation:

Weimaraner Breeder Report Card		
Source:		
Certificate/License:		
Website:		
Phone Number:		
Years Experience:		
Health Guarantee?	YES	NO
Puppies Available?	YES	NO
Colors Available?	Blue	Gray
Deposit Required?	YES	NO
Notes:		

Picking Out Healthy Weimaraner Puppies for Sale

Now that you've narrowed down your list of options for Weimaraner breeders, all you have to do is pick out your puppy! It is always best to actually visit the breeder and pick out your puppy in person – don't just pick a puppy based on a picture on a website. You want to interact with the puppies to get a feel for their temperaments and you want to be able to look them over to make sure they are in good health.

Picking out a Weimaraner puppy is no easy task – you need to be careful with your decision to make sure that your puppy is healthy and well-bred. Don't be duped by a backyard breeder!

When you get to the breeder, ask for a tour of the facilities if you haven't already had one. Make sure that the breeding stock looks to be in good health and that they are good specimens of the breed. If you have a preference for blue Weimaraner puppies over gray puppies, you should also make sure that the parents are the right color. If the puppies are less than 8 weeks old, you should also make sure that they are still with the mother because they need to be fully weaned before separation.

After making sure that the breeding stock are in good condition you can move on to the Weimaraner puppies for sale. Before you interact with the puppies, take a moment to stand back and observe them. Watch how the puppies interact with each other and be on the lookout for red flags like lethargic behavior, visible wounds, evidence of diarrhea, aggressive or fearful behavior, etc. As you observe the puppies, they should become aware of your presence and will probably wander over to you. Let the puppies sniff and explore you for a minute or two before you bend down to interact with them.

As you play with the Weimaraner puppies, make mental notes about each puppy in terms of his activity level, curiosity, and personality. Take turns petting each puppy and picking them up to take a quick physical exam. Observe how the puppy reacts to being picked up and see whether he is calm and seems to enjoy being held or if he appears to be very frightened of you (this could be a sign of poor socialization). Look the puppy over for signs of illness like discharge from the eyes or nose, visible wounds, dry flaky skin, patchy coat, or palpable masses under the skin.

Once you've had a chance to observe and interact with the puppies you should be ready to make your decision. If you know which puppy you want, tell the breeder and put down whatever deposit may be required to reserve the puppy – a responsible breeder won't sell a puppy less than 8 weeks old or one that hasn't been fully weaned. If the puppies are already weaned, you may be able to take your puppy home that very day.

CHAPTER 8

Your New Weimarane _____ppy

Puppy-Proofing, Toys, Supplies and More

B efore you bring your new Weimaraner puppy home, you need to make some preparations. Puppies are mischievous – especially Weimaraner puppies – so you need to make sure that your home is safe for your puppy. This is called puppy-proofing. You'll also need to stock up on some essential supplies and set up a special area of your home for your puppy to call his own.

What Supplies Does Your Weimaraner Puppy Need?

In order to meet your Weimaraner puppy's needs, you are going to need some basic supplies and necessities. Here is a list of what you'll need:

- A crate or kennel
- A dog bed or blanket
- Food and water bowls
- Chew toys
- Interactive toys
- Puppy playpen
- Grooming supplies

...ost important thing you need for your Weimaraner puppy ...his crate or kennel. While it may seem like confining a puppy to a crate is cruel, this is far from the truth. As long as you condition your puppy to think of the crate as his own personal space, he will actually like being in it! The key is to never use the crate as punishment. You should also spend a few days getting your puppy used to the crate by feeding him in it and by incorporating it into games during playtime.

Make sure that your Weimaraner puppy has plenty of toys to play with so he doesn't chew on your favorite shoes!

When choosing your puppy's crate, it needs to be fairly small - only large enough for your puppy to comfortably stand up, sit down, turn around, and lie down in. The idea is that if the crate is only large enough for your puppy to sleep in that he will come to think of it as his den. Dogs have a natural aversion to soiling their den so this will help immensely with housetraining. You can also line the crate with a bed or blanket to make it more comfortable for your Weimaraner puppy.

For food and water bowls, you want to choose something that is durable. The best choice for food and water bowls is usually stainless steel. Not only is stainless steel incredibly lightweight and durable, but it doesn't scratch or harbor bacteria like softer materials such as plastic can. If you don't like stainless steel, ceramic is another good option – just make sure that the bowls aren't too large or heavy. You'll be placing these bowls in your puppy's area which you will learn about in the next section.

In terms of toys for your Weimaraner puppy, you'll need a large assortment to start with so you can get a feel for what he likes. Choose several different kinds of chew toys to give your puppy an outlet for his natural desire to chew. You should also invest in some interactive toys to give your puppy some extra mental stimulation – this is especially important for intelligent breeds like the Weimaraner. If your puppy gets bored, he will likely resort to destructive behavior as a means of entertaining himself.

To keep your puppy contained, a puppy playpen is a great idea. If you have a puppy playpen you can keep your puppy from wandering around the house unsupervised without putting him in his crate. The playpen will become your puppy's own personal space when you place his crate inside as well as his food and water bowls and his favorite treats. Place the playpen in a room where it won't be in the way but won't be completely isolated. Once your puppy is housetrained, you may choose to put the playpen away and just keep his crate, bowls, and toys in the area so he has access to them.

You'll also want to have a collar, harness, and leash for your puppy. A Weimaraner dog collar needs to be sized for your puppy – this means that you'll have to buy several over the course of your dog's life or you can simply start with an adjustable collar. When it comes to the dog collar, Weimaraner dogs should always carry their ID tag as well as proof of their rabies vaccination. You may also want to think about a Weimaraner harness for your puppy. A harness helps to distribute pressure from the leash across the dog's back instead of concentrating it around his neck. It can also give you a little more control when your Weimaraner is fully grown.

Make sure that you have all the supplies you are going to need BEFORE you bring your Weimaraner puppy home.

Finally, you should invest in certain grooming supplies to have on hand for your Weimaraner puppy. Weimaraners have short coats, but they still need to be brushed a few times a week to control shedding. The perfect Weimaraner brush is a wire-pin brush with short bristles or you can just use a shedding rake. After brushing your Weimaraner's coat you can wipe it down with a chamois cloth to make it shine.

Puppy-Proofing – Keep Your Puppy Safe

In addition to setting up your puppy's own special area in the home, you should also go through the house and take steps to make sure that it is safe for puppy – this is called puppy proofing. It may help for you to walk around the house viewing things from your puppy's point of view to pick out potentially harmful things that could be tempting to play with. Here are some things that you should think about when puppy-proofing your house:

- Put away any cleaning products and various household chemicals in a cabinet that closes tightly or locks.
- Cover or put away open food containers in your cupboards or pantry.
- Cover your trash cans with tight-fitting lids or put them in a cabinet to keep your puppy out of them.
- Pick up all small objects off the floor and put them away where they belong.
- Wrap up electrical cords and blind cords so they don't dangle where your puppy can reach them.

- Keep medications and bathroom toiletries stowed safely away in a cabinet.

- Cover up open bodies of water like the bathtub and the toilet so your puppy doesn't fall in by accident.

- Check to be sure that none of your houseplants are poisonous and that they are out of puppy's reach.

- Close off your fireplace (if you have one) and make sure that all doors and windows stay tightly closed.

- Make sure that your puppy can't hurt himself on the furniture – avoid sharp edges and keep an eye out for rocking chairs.

- Use pet gates or baby gates to keep your puppy out of rooms that could be dangerous and to keep him away from the stairs.

- If you own a cat, make sure the litter box is kept somewhere your puppy can't reach– the same for pet food besides your puppy's own food.

- Pick up small clothing items (like socks and hosiery) and keep them out of your puppy's reach.

- Carefully dispose of food waste like fruit pits, vegetable peels, bones, etc.

CHAPTER 9

Feeding the Dog Weimaraner —
The Nutritional Needs of Weimaraners

Many dog owners assume that picking out a food for their dog is as simple as walking into a pet store and picking something off the shelf. What you may not realize, however, is that all dog foods are not created equal. I learned this the hard way. I used to feed my Misty a cheap store-brand dog food because it was inexpensive and she seemed to like it. After a few months on the food, however, I started to notice that she didn't have as much energy as she used to. Her coat was no longer shiny and she had frequent bouts of diarrhea. When I called my veterinarian, the first thing he asked was, "What are you feeding her?"

In this chapter, I'm going to tell you everything you need to know about your Weimaraner's nutritional needs. I'll also show you how to read a pet food label so you can make a comparison between products to pick the best one for your dog. You'll also receive tips for feeding your Weimaraner as a puppy and as an adult dog, plus a list of "people foods" to avoid feeding your Weimaraner.

What Nutrients Does Your Weimaraner Need?

Like all animals, dogs require a balance of protein, fat, and carbohydrate in their diet. Because dogs are largely carnivorous, protein is the most important of these three primary nutrients. Protein is what your Weimaraner puppy needs to develop strong muscles and healthy tissue. As you may already know, protein is made up of amino acids – these are often referred to as the "building blocks" of proteins. There are 22 different amino acids and your dog's body is capable of synthesizing, or creating, 12 of them. The remaining 10 amino acids are called essential amino acids because they come from your dog's diet.

Your Weimaraner needs a high-quality diet that is rich in animal protein and fat but low in carbohydrates with limited fiber.

When it comes to the protein content of your Weimaraner's diet, dogs require a minimum of 18% as adult dogs and

22% as puppies. The best protein sources for dogs are whole meats like poultry, beef, and fish as well as eggs. Animal proteins are not only easier for your dog's body to digest (because he is a carnivore and his body was made that way), but they are also complete proteins. A complete protein is one that contains all 10 essential amino acids. No matter what you choose to feed your pet, a high-quality animal protein needs to be the first ingredient.

The second most important nutrient in your Weimaraner's diet is fat. While you may have been raised to believe that fat is bad, it is actually highly essential for dogs. Not only is fat loaded with the essential fatty acids that help to maintain the condition of your dog's skin and coat, but it is also the most highly concentrated source of energy available to dogs. Like protein, fat should come from animal-based sources and it should make up a minimum of 8% a puppy's diet and 5% an adult dog's diet. Plant-based fats can be used in a supplemental way to balance out the omega-3 and omega-6 fatty acid content of your dog's diet.

When it comes to carbohydrates, dogs like the Weimaraner don't have any specific requirements. Carbohydrates provide your dog with usable energy as well as dietary fiber to help support his digestion. But a diet that is too carbohydrate-heavy can be bad for your dog. Your dog's body simply isn't designed to digest high quantities of plant-based foods. At the most, your dog's diet should contain 5% dietary fiber, though less is more. Any carbs in your dog's diet should also come from highly digestible sources like whole grains or fresh fruits and veggies.

You may need to be careful about picking a dog food that has grains in it, however. Grain like corn, wheat, and soy offer very little nutritional value for dogs and these are some of the most common food allergens. Whole grains like brown rice, oatmeal, and pearled barley are much better options in terms of nutrition but they can still cause problems for dogs that suffer from food allergies or sensitivities. Grain-free dog foods are usually made with starchy vegetables like potatoes or sweet potatoes – they may also include beans, legumes, or fresh veggies.

A balanced diet for Weimaraners will be protein-rich with healthy fats and natural sources for key vitamins and minerals.

To help balance out your Weimaraner's dog food, a high-quality product may also contain vitamin and mineral supplements. Natural sources for key nutrients (such as fresh fruits and vegetables) are always more digestible and more biologically valuable for dogs than synthetic supplements. Your dog's body can only absorb and utilize a portion of the nutrients in synthetic supplements. Chelated minerals are the best supplements to have because they have been chemically bonded to protein molecules which makes them easy for your dog's body to digest and absorb.

Tips for Reading a Dog Food Label

Now that you have a better understanding of what your Weimaraner's basic nutritional needs are, I can teach you how to read a pet food label so you can find a product that meets those needs. When you look at a pet food label it is easy to get distracted by colorful pictures of happy dogs. If you want to evaluate the quality of a product however, there are three places to look: the AAFCO statement of nutritional adequacy, the guaranteed analysis, and the ingredients list.

The American Association of Feed Control Officials (AAFCO) is responsible for regulating the production and manufacture of pet foods and animal feed. Essentially, this company does for pet food what the FDA and USDA do for human food. AAFCO has created nutrient profiles for adult dogs and puppies to determine their minimum nutritional requirements – they then compare each pet food product to those minimum requirements before they can be sold. If the product meets the minimum requirements, it is said to be "complete and balanced" for whatever life stage it is designed for (generally adult maintenance or puppies).

If the pet food label you are looking at carries this AAFCO statement, then you can rest assured that it will provide for your Weimaraner's minimum nutritional needs. Just because a product is "complete and balanced," however, doesn't necessarily mean that it is high quality. The next place you should look is the guaranteed analysis – the part of the label that tells you how much protein, fat, and fiber is in the product. Compare those values to the minimum requirements for dogs mentioned in the last section to see whether the product sticks to the bare minimum or if it exceeds the minimum.

Make sure that your Weimaraner' diet is properly balanced and made with high-quality ingredients like animal proteins and digestible carbohydrates – no by-products or fillers!

After you get a feel for the composition of the product by looking at the guaranteed analysis you should review the ingredients list to see if the product is made from quality ingredients. The first thing you need to remember is that ingredients lists are ordered in descending order by volume – whatever is at the top of the list is used in the highest volume.

This being the case, you want to see a high-quality protein as the first ingredient. Any product that lists a plant-based ingredient first should be avoided.

Within the top 10 ingredients on the list you want to see a high-quality protein first with supplemental proteins, healthy fats, and digestible carbohydrates. The order of these ingredients may vary but it is generally better to see the animal-based ingredients higher on the list than the plant-based ingredients. Again, you can refer to the guaranteed analysis to see how protein-rich the recipe is and to check the fiber content.

In terms of things you do NOT want to see on an ingredients list, avoid anything that includes the words "by-product" as well as anything made from corn, wheat, or soy. Products that are heavy with plant proteins (like pea protein or potato protein) are generally not high-quality products and anything with too many carbohydrates is best avoided. You also want to keep an eye out for artificial additives like colors, flavors, and preservatives.

Feeding Tips for Weimaraner Puppies and Adult Dogs

When it comes to how much you should be feeding your Weimaraner, recommendations vary according to several factors such as age, weight, sex, and activity level. Weimaraner puppies need a lot of energy and protein to fuel their growth, so consider a high-quality dog food that is formulated for medium to large-breed puppies. You may also be able to get away with a general puppy formula, though you do need to be mindful of the fat content for your Weimaraner puppy's diet. Excess fat can cause your puppy to grow very quickly and that is dangerous for larger dogs like the Weimaraner – it increases their risk for musculoskeletal problems when they grow up.

When feeding your Weimaraner puppy a large-breed puppy recipe, follow the feeding instructions on the label based on your puppy's age and weight. You may be able to let your Weimaraner puppy feed freely if he is able to ration himself, but if he starts to grow too quickly you should portion out his meals. Weigh your puppy at least once a week and talk to your vet if you are concerned.

Avoid feeding your Weimaraner too many treats because they can add up quickly and excess calories can lead to obesity in dogs.

Once your Weimaraner puppy reaches 80% of his expected adult size, you should switch over to an adult recipe – a large-breed adult recipe, in particular. These dog foods are usually high in protein with moderate fat content to prevent your dog from eating too many calories. Keep in mind that if you train your Weimaraner for hunting or dog sports, his energy needs may be higher. The best thing to do is to follow the feeding recommendations based on your dog's age, weight, and activity level for several weeks while tracking his weight. If he gains too much weight you can cut back a little bit and if he loses weight or energy, you can increase his portion a little bit.

Dangerous Foods to Avoid

Though it can be tempting to give in to your Weimaraner when he begs for table scraps, you need to be very careful. Many so-called "people foods" that you eat every day can actually be very dangerous for your dog. Here is a list of potentially harmful foods to avoid feeding your Weimaraner dog:

- Alcohol/beer
- Apple seeds
- Avocado
- Cherry pits
- Chocolate
- Coffee
- Garlic
- Grapes/raisins
- Macadamia nuts
- Mold
- Mushrooms
- Mustard seeds
- Onions/leeks
- Peach pits
- Potato leaves/stems
- Rhubarb leaves
- Tea
- Tomato leaves/stems
- Walnuts
- Xylitol
- Yeast dough

CHAPTER 10

Everything You Need to Know About Weimaraner Health

Every dog is susceptible to certain illnesses. Some of these diseases are inherited from the parent while others are related to anatomical abnormalities. Weimaraners are generally a healthy breed, but they are prone to certain diseases like any dog. In this chapter, you will learn about the most common health issues seen in the breed and you will learn about which vaccines your Weimaraner dog needs and when.

Common Health Problems in Weimaraner Dogs

When it comes to health problems affecting the Weimaraner breed, common issues can be divided into several categories. For musculoskeletal issues, Weimaraners are prone to hip and elbow dysplasia, hypertrophic osteodystrophy, and cervical spondylomyelopathy (also known as wobbler syndrome). For heart problems, these dogs are prone to dilated cardiomyopathy, atrial septal defects, tricuspid valve dysplasia, and patent ductus arteriosus. Other issues Weimaraners may face include eye problems, gastric torsion, autoimmune disease, and hypothyroidism.

To help protect your Weimaraner from these problems, you should learn as much as you can about them. Learning the basics about common health conditions affecting the breed can help you to identify symptoms when they manifest. The earlier you notice symptoms, he sooner you will be able to have your vet make a diagnosis and the sooner your dog can begin treatment. That is the key to the highest chances for a healthy recovery. Keep reading to learn the basics about common health problems affecting the Weimaraner dog breed.

The Weimaraner is a healthy breed by nature, although all dogs are prone to certain health problems. Weimaraners are particularly prone to musculoskeletal issues and heart problems.

Hip and Elbow Dysplasia

Hip and elbow dysplasia are both musculoskeletal issues known to affect medium to large-breed dogs like the Weimaraner. Hip dysplasia occurs when the head of the femur bone slips out of position in the hip socket. This can lead to pain or stiffness in the rear legs, as well as worsening arthritis. Elbow dysplasia is similar, resulting from a defect in the front legs of these dogs that causes the head of the humerus to slip out of place. Both of these conditions can be corrected surgically, though minor cases many only require medical management of symptoms.

Hypertrophic Osteodystrophy

This is a condition that commonly affects the front legs of medium to large-breed puppies like the Weimaraner. Hypertrophic osteodystrophy causes inflammation which leads to pain and severe lameness. The cause of this condition is still unknown, though it most commonly affects young dogs between 3 and 6 months of age. This disease causes swelling along the growth plates, difficulty moving, loss of appetite, and fever, as well as reluctance to move. It is generally treated with painkillers and anti-inflammatories – severe cases may require steroids.

Cervical Spondylomyelopathy

Also known as Wobbler Syndrome, cervical spondylomyelopathy is a condition of the cervical spine (the neck) that involves compression of the spinal cord, leading to neck pain and neurological symptoms. Symptoms of this condition may include wobbling gait, pain or stiffness in the neck, trouble walking, partial or complete paralysis, and difficulty rising from the ground. This condition is sometimes caused by excessive growth or malnutrition and it can be treated with surgery.

Dogs with dilated cardiomyopathy often experience exercise intolerance and may lose consciousness because blood isn't getting to the vital organs when and where it is needed.

Dilated Cardiomyopathy

This is a condition in which the heart is larger than normal and fails to function properly. Dilated cardiomyopathy may affect one side of the heart more than the other and it can affect the heart's ability to pump blood throughout the body. Without a regular supply of blood, the body begins to deteriorate and the lungs begin to fill with fluid. This condition usually affects Weimaraners between the age of 4 and 10 with common symptoms being lethargy, loss of appetite, shortness of breath, coughing, and loss of consciousness. The cause for this condition is unknown and treatment usually involves medication to manage the symptoms of the disease.

Atrial Septal Defects

An inherited heart anomaly, atrial septal defect is a condition in which blood flows between the left and right atria through the interatrial septum. When blood flows through the septum, it causes a volume overload in the right atrium as well as the right ventricle and pulmonary vasculature which can cause hypertension (high blood pressure). Common symptoms of this disease include fainting, exercise intolerance, trouble breathing, heart murmur, and fluid buildup in the abdomen.

Tricuspid Valve Dysplasia

A congenital heart defect, tricuspid valve dysplasia occurs when the tricuspid valve does not close as tightly as it should, allowing blood to leak backward through the valve. This is usually an inherited heart defect and the defect can vary in size. Puppies with a mild leak can still live a normal life but larger defects may be fatal before 1 year of age.

Patent Ductus Arteriosus

This condition involves a defect in the ductus arteriosus – the blood vessel that connects the pulmonary artery to the aorta in the heart. While puppies are still in the womb, this blood vessel helps to divert blood around the lungs because they are not needed yet. After birth, the vessel is supposed to close which allows blood to flow to the lungs. In cases of patent ductus arteriosus, however, this doesn't happen.

In cases of patent ductus arteriosus, some of the blood that is supposed to flow from the lungs through the heart and to the rest of the body ends up leaking back into the lungs. This causes the heart to work harder to pump blood and it can lead to early death if not treated. Treatment usually requires surgical correction of the problem.

Some Weimaraners struggle with ear infections because their large, floppy ears prevent air from getting to the ear canal.

Eye Problems

Weimaraner dogs are prone to a number of eye problems including distichiasis, entropion, and corneal dystrophy. Distichiasis occurs when extra eyelashes begin to grow from an abnormal location on the eyelid. Depending where the eyelashes grow from, they could touch the surface of the eye, causing irritation or even abrasion. This condition can be painful and treatment may require manual removal of the extra lashes.

Entropion is a condition in which the eyelid rolls inward, causing the eyelashes or hairs on the surface to rub against the cornea. Similar to distichiasis, this condition can lead to minor irritation or abrasion which may require surgical correction. Corneal dystrophy involves the formation of white, opaque mineral deposits in the cornea of the eye. This is generally an inherited condition, though it may also be due to high cholesterol or blood calcium levels. Treatment may involve topical medications and dietary management. Severe cases may require surgical correction.

Gastric Torsion

Also known as gastric dilation volvulus, gastric torsion is a condition that commonly affects large and deep-chested dog breeds. This condition occurs when the abdomen begins to fill with air, causing the stomach to twist on its axis. This cuts off blood supply to the stomach and other vital organs which can quickly result in an emergency situation. Without emergency veterinary attention, most dogs die of this condition. To help prevent bloat, keep your dog from eating or drinking large quantities at once, especially after exercise.

Autoimmune Disease

An autoimmune disease is a condition in which the body's own immune system begins attacking healthy cells and tissues. Depending which organ or bodily system is affected by the disorder, autoimmune disease can be very serious – even deadly. Autoimmune disease can affect the blood, the skin, the joints, the glands, the digestive system, or other parts of the body. There is no known cause yet for autoimmune disease in dogs, though it may be triggered by vaccines, environmental pollutants, preservatives, stress, or various infections.

The exact cause for autoimmune disease in dogs is unknown and it can manifest in a variety of different ways.

Hypothyroidism

Hypothyroidism is caused by inadequate output of thyroid hormone by the thyroid gland. This may be the result of damage to the thyroid gland, frequently caused by autoimmune activity or cancer – it can also be related to the use of certain medications. A mild deficiency in thyroid hormone output generally doesn't cause much problem or result in noticeable symptoms but this is a condition that requires lifelong treatment with synthetic hormone supplements.

Symptoms of hypothyroidism in Weimaraners may include thinning coat, course or brittle hair, lethargy, drooping eyelids, mental dullness, unexplained weight gain and irregular heat cycles in female dogs. This condition can affect dogs of any age, though it is most common in middle-aged dogs 4 to 10 years old. Although lifelong treatment is required for hypothyroidism, once treatment is started, the symptoms usually clear up and the dog is fine.

Recommended Vaccinations for Weimaraners

In the same way that you get vaccinated against the flu each year, your Weimaraner also needs certain annual vaccines. As a puppy, your Weimaraner probably received certain vaccines every 6 to 12 weeks during his first year of life. After that first year, most vaccines only need to be given as an annual booster. The vaccines your dog needs depend on his age and where you live – your veterinarian will be able to tell you what your dog needs.

To give you an idea exactly which vaccines your Weimaraner might need and when, here is a schedule for dog vaccinations:

Vaccination Schedule for Dogs			
Vaccine	Doses	Age	Booster
Rabies (US only)	1	12 weeks	annual
Distemper	3	6-16 weeks	3 years
Parvovirus	3	6-16 weeks	3 years
Adenovirus	3	6-16 weeks	3 years
Parainfluenza	3	6 weeks, 12-14 weeks	3 years
Bordetella	1	6 weeks	annual
Lyme Disease	2	9, 13-14 weeks	annual
Leptospirosis	2	12 and 16 weeks	annual
Canine Influenza	2	6-8, 8-12 weeks	annual

CHAPTER 11

Weimaraner Training –

A Complete Guide to Dog Training for Weimaraners

One of your most important tasks as a Weimaraner dog owner is to train your dog. Puppy training and dog training is not complicated, as dog training books sometimes make it seem – all you really need to know is the basics of positive reinforcement and you'll be able to teach your Weimaraner to do just about anything. In this chapter, you'll learn the basics about Weimaraner dog training, including tips for crate training and dog clicker training.

The Dos and Don'ts of Weimaraner Dog Training

In order to understand how to train a puppy or how to train a dog, you first need to understand a little bit about dog behavior. Dogs are generally predictable animals – they are motivated by food and by the desire to please their owners. If you can show your Weimaraner that performing a certain behavior makes you happy, he will be eager to repeat it – more so if you give him a food reward for doing so. Weimaraners are like any other dog in that they love to eat, so food rewards are highly motivating for this breed.

Another thing you need to remember about dog training is that you have to be consistent. An effective dog trainer will use the same commands consistently and he will also be consistent in issuing praise and reward. If you want your dog to do something, you have to praise him for doing it – each and every time. You can phase out food rewards after your dog gets the hang of the training sequence so he doesn't become dependent on the treats, but he still needs to know that you approve of his behavior.

The Weimaraner is an incredibly intelligent and people-oriented breed – he WANTS to do what you what him to do!

In terms of what you should NOT do with dog obedience training, is to never punish your dog for doing something wrong. There is an old dog training method that says if your dog has an accident on the rug and you rub his nose in it, he will learn not to have an accident in the house. Not only is this incredibly incorrect but it is also a dangerous habit to get into. Unless the punishment immediately follows the crime, your dog is unlikely to connect the punishment to any particular behavior – he will just understand that you are being mean to him and it could have a negative impact on your bond with your dog.

It may also be helpful for you to learn that problem behaviors in dogs are often completely natural behaviors – they only become a problem when you don't like the way those behaviors manifest. For example, puppies chew on things because they are exploring their world with their mouths – they don't have hands so they pick things up in their mouth to see what they are. This becomes a problem behavior for you when your puppy does it to your shoes, or to something else you don't want him chewing on.

The best way to deal with so-called problem behaviors in dogs is to redirect the unwanted behavior toward a more appropriate outlet. For example, if your Weimaraner puppy is chewing on your favorite shoe you should take the show away and tell him "No" in a firm tone of voice. Then, immediately give him one of his chew toys and praise him when he starts to chew on that instead. This way your puppy will learn what he can and cannot chew on and you won't have to punish him.

Crate Training Your Weimaraner Puppy

One of your first training challenges as a Weimaraner dog

trainer is to tackle the task of housetraining. Housetraining a puppy is not a particularly difficult task, but it does take some time and patience. Basically, you want to teach your Weimaraner puppy that you like it when he does his business outdoors. If you praise him and reward him for doing this, that is what he will learn to do. You'll also need to supervise him when you are at home to prevent him from having an accident in the house.

Housetraining a puppy is much easier than most people think — you just must be consistent about letting your puppy out and making sure he knows where he is supposed to go.

When you are potty training a puppy, it will help to have a crate or at least a puppy playpen where you can keep your Weimaraner puppy confined while you can't physically keep an eye on him. When you are able to watch your puppy, keep him in the same room with you at all times so you can keep a watch for signs that he has to go. If your puppy starts to sniff the ground, turn in circles, or squat, it is time to pick him up and rush him outside.

While you are housetraining a puppy, you should take your puppy outside at least once every hour or two. He will also need to go immediately after waking from a nap, before going to bed at night, and about 30 minutes after a meal. When you take your Weimaraner puppy outside, always take him to the same location, so he learns that is where he is expected to do his business. When he does, praise him excitedly so he knows that you approve. You can also try giving him a verbal command like "Go Pee" when you take him to his spot – eventually you'll be able to just open the door, give him the command, and he'll know what to do.

By supervising your puppy when he is awake and keeping him in his crate while he is asleep, you can drastically reduce the risk for accidents in the house – that is the key to potty training a puppy. Just be as consistent as possible with giving your puppy chances to go outside and don't force him to hold his bladder for longer than he is able. Puppies can only control their bladder and bowels for about 1 hour per month of age, plus one. So, a two-month old Weimaraner puppy can only hold his bladder for a maximum of about 3 hours.

Positive Reinforcement/Clicker Training

The second most important aspect of dog training for your Weimaraner is dog obedience training – teaching your dog to respond to certain commands. You've already learned the basics of positive reinforcement for dog training – you just show your dog what you want him to do and then reward him for doing it. Smart dogs like the Weimaraner usually pick up on things pretty quickly, so it may only take three or four repetitions for your dog to catch on.

If your Weimaraner is having trouble with dog obedience training, you might consider enrolling him in dog training classes. Obedience classes for puppies can be a lot of fun for both you and your dog – plus they double as a socialization opportunity. Obedience school for dogs works best when the owner accompanies the dog – if you hire a dog trainer your Weimaraner will learn to respond to his commands but may not respond to yours. You will want to do the training yourself for the best results.

Something else that might help you with dog obedience training for Weimaraners is clicker training. This is simply another type of positive reinforcement training that can help your dog identify the desired behavior. That is the key to training – you give your dog a command and teach him what response you expect for that command. When your dog shows the proper response, you immediately praise him and reward him to reinforce it. With clicker training, you click a little sound maker as soon as your dog performs the desired behavior, which helps him to identify it more quickly. After three or four repetitions your dog will catch on and you can stop using the clicker.

CHAPTER 12

Weimaraner Grooming:

Tips for Keeping Your Weimaraner Dog Looking His Absolute Best

A high-quality and healhty diet will keep your Weimaraner feeling his best, but you'll need to do some occasional grooming to have him looking his best. The Weimaraner's coat is fairly short which makes it easy to take care of and you don't have to worry about trimming it. You do, however, need to brush your dog to control shedding, and you'll also need to care for his teeth, toenails, and ears.

What is the Weimaraner's Coat Like?

The Weimaraner is known for his silver-blue coat, though it technically comes in a range of different tones. Some Weimaraners are silver to the point of almost being blue while others have more of a brown tone to their coats. It all depends on genetics and breeding which determines color and coat type.

The Weimaraner's coat is generally short and fairly dense with a smooth texture. When your dog gets enough healthy fats in his diet, this coat will also have a natural shine. You can also wipe the coat with a chamois to make it shinier. Because the coat is short, you don't need to brush it very often – once or twice a week is usually sufficient. These dogs do shed, but not as much as breeds with longer and thicker coats. Some Weimaraners do have longer coats with a fuller tail, but the short coat is standard.

Weimaraners love to get down and dirty when they play outside so be sure to keep a bottle of dog shampoo handy!

Brushing and Bathing Your Weimaraner

Taking care of your Weimaraner's coat is fairly easy, because all you really need is a wire pin brush or a slicker brush. To keep shedding under control, brush your Weimaraner's coat thoroughly about once a week. Start at the back of your dog's head near the base of his neck and gently work your way down the back and sides, moving the brush in the direction of hair growth. The Weimaraner's coat is short enough that you shouldn't have to worry about tangles and mats, but be careful anyway.

After working through your dog's back, focus on the legs – keep moving in the direction of hair growth. Work slowly down each leg, then have your Weimaraner lie down so you can brush his belly and chest. Some dogs don't like the feel of the brush, but most of them do, as long as you are gentle. If your Weimaraner is nervous about it, you can work with him slowly and keep your grooming sessions short so that you don't overwhelm him.

The Weimaraner's coat is fairly dense so it naturally repels dirt and dust. If your Weimaraner spends a lot of time outside, however, he may still need the occasional bath. The best way to bathe your Weimaraner is to fill a bathtub with a few inches of warm water (not hot) and have your dog step into it. Use a cup or a handheld sprayer to wet down your dog's coat then apply a small amount of dog-friendly shampoo and work it into a lather.

After you've lathered up your Weimaraner, rinse him thoroughly to remove all traces of soap. Be careful to avoid getting your dog's face or ears wet because wetness inside the ears can become a breeding ground for bacteria. If you need to clean your dog's face and head, use a damp washcloth and be very careful. Once your dog is clean, remove as much moisture as you can with a towel then finish him off with a blow-dryer on the low heat setting if your dog will allow it. If it is warm outside, you can also let your Weimaraner air-dry as long as he doesn't go rolling in something to ruin his nice clean coat.

Other Grooming Tasks – Clipping and Trimming

In addition to brushing and bathing your Weimaraner, you also need to take care of his teeth, toenails, and ears. Weimaraners have flop ears which means that they hang down on either side of his head instead of standing erect. Flop ears get less air flow than erect ears which increases the dog's risk for ear infections – you need to keep your Weimaraner's ears clean and dry. Luckily, cleaning your dog's ears is very easy.

Before you trim your Weimaraner's nails for the first time it isn't a bad idea to have a vet or professional groomer show you how.

To clean your Weimaraner's ears, simply squeeze a few drops of dog-safe ear cleaner into the ear canal and then carefully massage the base of your dog's ear to distribute the solution. Use a clean cotton ball or cotton swab to remove ear wax and debris along with any excess solution. Then just let your dog's ears air-dry. It only takes a few minutes but it goes a long way toward preventing painful ear infections.

Cleaning your Weimaraner's teeth is equally important but it is a little bit trickier. The key to brushing your dog's teeth is to get him used to it as a puppy. Start by getting your puppy used to having his face, mouth, and teeth touched. You can use your fingers at first and gradually work your way up to using a dog-safe tooth brush. Once your puppy is used to the tooth brush you can add some dog-friendly tooth paste and brush a few teeth at a time. Slowly work your way up to brushing all the top teeth or all of the bottom teeth in one session and do it as often as your Weimaraner will let you.

The last grooming task you need to worry about for Weimaraner dogs is trimming the nails. If your Weimaraner spends a lot of time outside, his nails might get worn down naturally but you should still check them. Overgrown nails can become brittle and break, which could be painful for your dog. It is also possible for the nail to grow so long that it starts to curve back into your dog's paw. Trimming the nails every week or two will prevent this from happening.

Trimming your Weimaraner's nails is pretty easy, but you

should probably have a vet or groomer show you how to do it the first time. Your dog's nail contains a blood vessel called the quick which provides the blood supply to the nail – it is the darker, reddish portion of the lower nail. If you cut your dog's nail too short, you could sever the quick – this will not only be painful for your dog but it will likely cause profuse bleeding as well. The best thing to do is to trim minimum amount from your Weimaraner's nails every week or two to prevent overgrowth.

CHAPTER 13

Weimaraner Life Expectancy and Caring for Older Weimaraner Dogs

They say that dog is a man's best friend and that has certainly been true of myself and my Misty. As wonderful a friend as Misty has been for the past few years, I know that my time with her is limited. Weimaraners are large dogs so they only live to an average lifespan of 10 to 12 years, though some have lived 15 years or more. As my dog gets older, I will have to make certain accommodations to keep her comfortable. You will have to do the same for your Weimaraner.

Each year you spend with your Weimaraner is better than the one before. Unfortunately, it also means that your Weimaraner is one year closer to the end of his lifespan. What many people do not realize is that a dog's life is in fast-forward compared to that of a human. Weimaraner puppies grow very quickly for the first year or two but once they reach maturity, their growth and aging occurs at a slower rate. Still, your dog will age more quickly than you which is why his lifespan is so much shorter.

To give you an idea of what this looks like, here is an age chart for human years and how it correlated with your Weimaraner dog's age:

Calendar Year	Weimaraner Age Equivalent
1 Year	15
2 Years	24
3 Years	29
4 Years	34
5 Years	39
6 Years	44
7 Years	48
8 Years	53
9 Years	58
10 Years	63
11 Years	68
12 Years	73
13 Years	78
14 Years	83
15 Years	88

How long your Weimaraner is going to live will be determined by a number of factors. For one thing, responsible breeding plays a major role – if your Weimaraner's parents were healthy and long-lived, your dog might be as well. If your Weimaraner was poorly bred or affected by any inherited diseases, it could seriously reduce his longevity. Even seemingly minor health problems can affect your dog's lifespan.

One of the biggest determining factors in your dog's health (and therefore his longevity) is the quality of his diet. You have already learned about your Weimaraner's nutritional needs, but you need to take these needs very seriously. If you skimp on your dog's diet and feed him a dog food that isn't high-quality, it could lead to a number of health problems such as malnutrition, nutritional deficiencies, and various diseases, all of which could limit his lifespan. It may cost more to buy a high-quality dog food in the short term, but it will save you on expensive vet bills in the long term. Isn't it worth it to keep your dog healthy?

Dogs age much more quickly than humans so you should start thinking about geriatric care when your dog is 7 years old.

As your Weimaraner gets older, you need to make some adjustments to his lifestyle. Technically, a Weimaraner reaches "old age" around the 7-year mark. If you aren't already taking your dog to the vet for two check-ups a year, you should start doing it now. Your vet will help you decide if you are feeding your dog enough and if it is the right kind of food. He will also help you determine how much and what kind of exercise is safe for your dog. Regular check-ups are also the key to catching diseases and health problems in the early stages.

In addition to keeping up with routine vet check-ups, you should also take steps to make sure that your aging Weimaraner is comfortable. If your dog develops bone or joint problems, consider buying him an orthopedic pet bed to provide support. Ask your vet if supplements like glucosamine and chondroitin might also be beneficial. Don't let your Weimaraner spend too much time outside when it is particularly hot or cold, and avoid exposing him to extreme temperatures and inclement weather.

As your Weimaraner gets older, he may start to have accidents in the house. For many dogs, incontinence is just a consequence of aging. It is possible, however, that it could be a symptom of disease, so bring it up with your vet if it comes on suddenly. You may also want to give your Weimaraner a raised bowl so he doesn't have to strain himself bending down and invest in a ramp or set of stairs to help your dog get in and out of the car.

CHAPTER 14

Things to Think About Before Showing Your Weimaraner

I f you have ever watched the Westminster Kennel Club show on television, you probably know that dog shows are a pretty big deal. Hundreds of dog owners enter the biggest dog show competitions each year, all with the hopes of earning the honor of "Best in Show". But showing your Weimaraner is not easy – it takes a lot of time and discipline, especially if you want to do well. In this chapter, you will learn about some of the reasons to consider showing your dog and you'll receive tips for making the most of your first show.

Why Should You Consider Showing Your Weimaraner?

When it comes to dog shows, there are several reasons why you might consider entering your dog. For one thing, the possibility of your dog being name "Best in Show" comes with a great deal of honor – both for you and for the breeder. This is by far the best award, but there are also lesser prizes that you could win such as "Best in Class" or "Best of Breed".

In addition to the potential for an amazing prize, showing

your Weimaraner can be enjoyable as well as challenging. Preparing your dog for show and working with him in training can help the two of you grow closer together. Weimaraners love having a job to do and they are very eager to please their owners, so if you enjoy working with your dog, he will enjoy preparing for show. All that training is also great for teaching your dog discipline and reinforcing his obedience.

If you plan to show your Weimaraner, make sure he is a good example of the breed standard published by whatever dog breed organization is running that particular show.

Another thing that you might enjoy about dog shows is the opportunity to work alongside other dog lovers. A dog show is a great place to build a network of fellow dog lovers, and not just other Weimaraner owners! You can learn a lot just by going to a dog show, even if you don't compete. And dog owners love to talk about their dogs, so don't be shy about asking questions!

Simple Tips for Your First Dog Show

You cannot just show up at a dog show and expect your Weimaraner to win. It takes a lot of time to prepare for a show and there are certain things you need to do on the day of the show. The more often you and your dog compete, the more you will learn and the better you will do. <u>Here are some simple tips for making the most of your first dog show:</u>

- Avoid feeding your Weimaraner too much on the day of the show – you want them to be hungry enough to perform for food in the show ring.

- Arrive at the show at least an hour early so you have time to set up, walk the dog, and get your bearings.

- Keep your Weimaraner in his crate when he isn't eating or doing his business – you want him to be in tip-top shape and appearance for judging.

- Make sure your dog is ready to go at least a few minutes before the appointed time – you want to be able to hand him off to the handler when it's his turn.

- Take plenty of pictures and notes about your experience to use in preparing for the next show.

- Keep a positive mindset throughout the experience, even if your dog doesn't do well – learn from your mistakes for next time!

  Have fun! A dog show can be an exciting challenge, but it should also be fun for both you and your dog.

CHAPTER 15

Breeding Weimaraners – Is it Really the Best Choice for Your Dog?

There is nothing cuter than a Weimaraner puppy - that is just a fact of life. But raising a Weimaraner puppy can be very challenging, so just think of what it would be like to care for a whole litter of them! Dog breeding often sounds like a great idea until you buckle down and think about the details. Can you commit to responsible breeding practices like DNA testing? Can you financially support the veterinary needs of a pregnant female and a whole litter of puppies? Are you prepared to lose money or (the best-case scenario) break even on selling the puppies? These are all questions you need to ask yourself before breeding your Weimaraner.

What Does it Take to Breed Dogs?

Before you decide whether to breed your Weimaraner, you should take the time to learn how dog breeding works and what you will have to do. For one thing, you are going to need two Weimaraner adults (a male and a female), both in excellent health and condition. Once you have your dogs, you'll need to have them DNA tested to see if they are carriers for any inherited health problems like hip dysplasia, hypothyroidism, and tricuspid dysplasia (a heart problem). If either of the dogs is a carrier, he or she should not be bred.

Nothing is cuter than a litter of Weimaraner puppies – the average litter size for this breed is 6 to 8 puppies.

After you've done the DNA testing, then comes the task of preparing your dogs for breeding as well as the actual breeding process. Your dogs need to be in tip-top shape in terms of their health and fitness. If you try to breed a female Weimaraner who is in less than optimal health, the stress and strain of the pregnancy could become dangerous. You'll need to keep a close eye on her health throughout the gestation period with frequent visits to the vet. You'll also have to deal with her changing energy needs, making sure that she has access to high-quality food in the right quantities to support the development of the puppies.

Once the puppies are born, your job gets even harder. Not only are your caring for a post-partum female dog but you are also responsible for the growth and development of a litter of puppies. Weimaraners have an average litter size of 6 to 8 puppies – can you handle that? Not only will you need to make sure that the mother stays in good health so she can produce milk for the puppies, but you also need to make sure that they get a health check-up and that they get their puppy shots. You'll have to care for the puppies until they are at least 8 weeks old and completely weaned before you can sell them.

Understanding the Heat Cycle for Dogs

If you are sure that you want to breed your Weimaraner, you'll need to know how the breeding process works. Because Weimaraners are a large-breed dog, they take a little longer to mature than larger breeds. While many female dogs experience their first heat around 6 months of age, female Weimaraners generally don't become sexually mature until closer to 12 months. The heat cycle is simply the biological cycle through which a female dog becomes capable of and receptive to breeding. If a female dog in heat is successfully mated to a fertile male, it will result in pregnancy, which starts the gestation period.

The heat cycle in dogs is more commonly known as the estrous cycle and it consists of several stages. The length of the cycle may vary from one breed to another but in Weimaraners it is usually about 18 days. The first stage, proestrous, lasts for an average of 9 days and this is when your female dog will start bleeding. At this point she will be attractive to male dogs but not ready for breeding. The estrous stage is next – it lasts about 9 days as well and it is the stage in which the female becomes receptive to the male. If the female is bred successfully, she will conceive and start the gestation period.

Dogs are diestrous animals – this means that they generally go into heat twice a year. As a larger breed, however, the Weimaraner may only have one heat per year – it just depends on the female.

The gestation period is the period of time following conception during which the fetuses develop in the dog's womb. For most dogs, the gestation period lasts about 63 days (or 9 weeks). As the puppies grow inside the mother's womb, she will need to eat a little bit more to support the nutritional needs of the puppies on top of her own. Generally, you can just leave a bowl of food for your female Weimaraner and she will eat as much as she needs – it is better to let her eat a little more than she needs than to not give her enough food. Near the end of the gestation period she may be eating two or three times as much as she was prior to pregnancy.

Near the end of the gestation period, you will notice that your female Weimaraner starts to get restless – this is a sign of impending labor. At this point you should have a whelping box prepared for your dog in a quiet, dim location where she can give birth in peace. Do whatever you can to keep your Weimaraner comfortable at this time, but know that labor is just as painful for dogs as it is for humans. Soothe your dog as she cries and pet her gently, making sure that she knows you are by her side.

When your Weimaraner is ready to give birth, her water will break and she will start whelping the puppies. The puppies will probably come about ten minutes apart and the mother may or may not clean each puppy off before the next one comes. If your dog doesn't sever the umbilical cords herself, snip the cord with a pair of sanitized scissors. After all of the puppies have been born, the mother will deliver the afterbirth – if she doesn't eat it, just throw it away. It is normal for dogs to eat the afterbirth because it is very rich in nutrients.

After the puppies have been delivered, the female Weimaraner will do most of the work in caring for them. The puppies will be completely dependent on their mother for food and warmth for several weeks but the will eventually become active as their ears and eyes open. The puppies may be ready to start sampling moistened dry food after a few weeks and they should be completely weaned around 7 to 8 weeks.

CHAPTER 16

Conclusion

I f you want to know the truth, I absolutely believe that the Weimaraner is the best dog breed out there. The only thing I regret about having my Misty is that I waited so long to get her! I can't believe that I was living in a world where I didn't know Weimaraners existed and I can't imagine going back. That is exactly why I wrote this book – to share my love for Weimaraners with the world, in hopes of convincing others that these are the best dogs out there!

Although I've spent a lot of time talking about how great the Weimaraner breed is in this book, I want to make sure I touch on an equally important point – owning a dog is time-consuming and it can be expensive as well. Weimaraners can live from 10 to 12 years so they are by no means a short-term commitment! Throughout your Weimaraner's life, you will be responsible for feeding, walking, and training him as well as providing for his other needs. You are his parent, not just his companion!

The Weimaraner is not only one of the friendliest and most

people-oriented breeds you will come across - he is also very smart and absolutely gorgeous. Just look at that silver-blue coat! Keep in mind that Weimaraners are a fairly high-maintenance breed in terms of energy, space, and attention requirements. They do not shed a great deal, however, and their coats are easy to groom.

Nothing is more adorable than a Weimaraner puppy – just look at those big floppy ears and those sad eyes!

If you haven't decided by now that the Weimaraner is the right breed for you and your family, you probably never will. There is nothing wrong with that! As much as I love Weimaraners I understand that they are not the right fit for everyone, but if you are looking for a gentle, devoted family pet, this might be the right choice.

Thanks for taking the time to read this book – I hope you've come to love the Weimaraner breed as much as I do! If you have even the slightest notion that the Weimaraner is a dog breed worth considering, I have done my job. So, good luck and God bless you and your new Weimaraner!

Useful Terms to Know

AKC – American Kennel Club, the largest purebred dog registry in the United States

Almond Eye – Referring to an elongated eye shape rather than a rounded shape

Apple Head – A round-shaped skull

Balance – A show term referring to all of the parts of the dog, both moving and standing, which produce a harmonious image

Beard – Long, thick hair on the dog's underjaw

Best in Show – An award given to the only undefeated dog left standing at the end of judging

Bitch – A female dog

Bite – The position of the upper and lower teeth when the dog's jaws are closed; positions include level, undershot, scissors, or overshot

Blaze – A white stripe running down the center of the face between the eyes

Board – To house, feed, and care for a dog for a fee

Breed – A domestic race of dogs having a common gene pool and characterized appearance/function

Breed Standard – A published document describing the look, movement, and behavior of the perfect specimen of a particular breed

Buff – An off-white to gold coloring

Clip – A method of trimming the coat in some breeds

Coat – The hair covering of a dog; some breeds have two coats, and outer coat and undercoat; also known as a double coat. Examples of breeds with double coats include

German Shepherd, Siberian Husky, Akita, etc.

Condition – The health of the dog as shown by its skin, coat, behavior, and general appearance

Crate – A container used to house/transport dogs; also called a cage or kennel

Crossbreed (Hybrid) – A dog having a sire and dam of two different breeds; cannot be registered with the AKC

Dam (bitch) – The female parent of a dog;

Dock – To shorten the tail of a dog by surgically removing the end part of the tail.

Double Coat – Having an outer weather-resistant coat and a soft, waterproof coat for warmth; see above.

Drop Ear – An ear in which the tip of the ear folds over and hangs down; not prick or erect

Entropion – A genetic disorder resulting in the upper or lower eyelid turning in

Fancier – A person who is especially interested in a particular breed or dog sport

Fawn – A red-yellow hue of brown

Feathering – A long fringe of hair on the ears, tail, legs, or body of a dog

Groom – To brush, trim, comb or otherwise make a dog's coat neat in appearance

Heel – To command a dog to stay close by its owner's side

Hip Dysplasia – A condition characterized by the abnormal formation of the hip joint

Inbreeding – The breeding of two closely related dogs of one breed

Kennel – A building or enclosure where dogs are kept

Litter – A group of puppies born at one time

Markings – A contrasting color or pattern on a dog's coat

Mask – Dark shading on the dog's foreface

Mate – To breed a dog and a bitch

Neuter – To castrate a male dog or spay a female dog

Pads – The tough, shock-absorbent skin on the bottom of a dog's foot

Parti-Color – A coloration of a dog's coat consisting of two or more definite, well-broken colors; one of the colors must be white

Pedigree – The written record of a dog's genealogy going back three generations or more

Pied – A coloration on a dog consisting of patches of white and another color

Prick Ear – Ear that is carried erect, usually pointed at the tip of the ear

Puppy – A dog under 12 months of age

Purebred – A dog whose sire and dam belong to the same breed and who are of unmixed descent

Saddle – Colored markings in the shape of a saddle over the back; colors may vary

Shedding – The natural process whereby old hair falls off the dog's body as it is replaced by new hair growth.

Sire – The male parent of a dog

Smooth Coat – Short hair that is close-lying

Spay – The surgery to remove a female dog's ovaries, rendering her incapable of breeding

Trim – To groom a dog's coat by plucking or clipping

Undercoat – The soft, short coat typically concealed by a longer outer coat

Wean – The process through which puppies transition from subsisting on their mother's milk to eating solid food

Whelping – The act of birthing a litter of puppies

Index

29, 30, 31, 32, 33, 34, 35, 48, 50, 53, 67, 69, 71, 72, 73, 81, 82, 98, 100, 101, 102, 103, 106, 107, 108, 109, 110, 111

breeder · 14, 40, 41, 42, 43, 47, 48, 49, 50, 51, 52, 54, 97

breeding · 110, 111

breeding stock · 50, 51, 52, 53

brush · 13, 29, 59, 87, 88, 89, 91, 110

by-product · 67

C

cage · 110

calories · 68, 69

Canine Influenza · 80

carbohydrate · 62, 63

cardiomyopathy · 74

care · 109

caring · 16, 102, 105

carnivore · 63

carrier · 101

castrate · 111

cats · 33

cause · 28, 64, 68, 73, 75, 78, 79, 92

certifications · 49

cervical spondylomyelopathy · 71, 73

challenge · 18, 32, 34, 99

chamois · 59, 88

chewing · 83

cleaning products · 59

clicker training · 81, 86

club · 20, 48

coat · 13, 15, 19, 20, 23, 24, 43, 53, 59, 61, 63, 79, 87, 88, 89, 90, 107, 109, 110, 111

coat color · 13

collar · 58

color · 23, 24, 25, 43, 53, 87, 110, 111

coloration · 24, 111

coloring · 109

colors · 111

comb · 110

command · 33, 34, 85, 86, 110

complete protein · 63

condition · 49, 51, 53, 56, 63, 73, 74, 75, 76, 77, 78, 79, 100, 110

consistent · 32, 34, 82, 84, 85

cords · 59, 104

corneal dystrophy · 77

costs · 38

crate · 55, 56, 57, 81, 84, 85, 99

crossbreeding · 27

cycle · 102

D

dam · 110, 111

dangerous · 60, 68, 69, 83, 101

deficiencies · 95

deposit · 14, 50, 54

designer dog · 26

destructive · 38, 39, 40, 57

development · 20, 24, 102

diagnosis · 4, 72

diarrhea · 53, 61

diet · 62, 63, 64, 66, 68, 87, 95

dietary fiber · 63

digestion · 63

dilated cardiomyopathy · 71, 74

guaranteed analysis · 65, 66, 67

H

hair · 109, 110, 111

harness · 58

health · 4, 31, 50, 52, 71, 72, 94, 95, 96, 100, 101, 102, 110

health issues · 71

healthy · 16, 48, 52, 62, 64, 67, 71, 72, 78, 87, 94, 95

heart · 29, 49, 71, 72, 74, 75, 76, 101

heart defect · 75

heart problems · 71, 72

heat · 79, 89, 102, 103

hip · 110

Hip Dysplasia · 110

history · 17, 19

house · 109, 110

houseplants · 60

housetrain · 38

housetraining · 57, 84, 85

hunting · 14, 15, 19, 20, 22, 30, 33, 69

hypertrophic osteodysrophy · 71

hypothyroidism · 72, 79, 101

I

illness · 53

immune system · 78

independent · 32, 33, 41

inexpensive · 61

infections · 76, 78, 90, 91

inflammation · 73

information · 2, 3, 16, 17, 18, 23, 26, 32, 42

ingredient · 63, 67

inherited · 71, 75, 77, 94, 101

intelligence · 15, 34

irritation · 77

J

joint · 96, 110

K

kennel · 110

kennels · 45, 46, 47

kids · 32

L

labor · 104

Labrador Retriever · 27

lameness · 73

leadership · 34

leash · 58

legs · 13, 17, 24, 25, 73, 89, 110

Leptospirosis · 80

lethargic · 53

lethargy · 75, 79

lifespan · 93, 94, 95

lips · 23

litter · 48, 60, 100, 101, 102, 111

long haired · 24, 25

love · 13

loyal · 31

lungs · 75, 76

M

male · 111

malnutrition · 47, 74, 95

vitamin · 64

W

water · 55, 57, 60, 89, 104

WCA · 48

weaned · 53, 54, 102, 105

weight · 67, 68, 69, 79

Weimar · 19

Weimaraner Club of America · 12, 19, 21, 25, 26, 48

Weimaraner Club of Great Britain · 12, 48

Weimaraner Lab mix · 27

Weimaraner mix · 26, 27

Westminster Kennel Club · 21, 97

white · 109, 111

whole grains · 63

wobbler syndrome · 71, 73

womb · 76, 103

work · 3, 4, 15, 16, 30, 38, 76, 89, 91, 98, 105

wounds · 53

Y

yard · 17

Made in the USA
Middletown, DE
24 February 2020